Energy for Today

Oil, Gas, and Coal

By Tea Benduhn

Reading consultant: Susan Nations, M.Ed.,
author/literacy coach/consultant in literacy development

Science and curriculum consultant: Debra Voege, M.A.,
science curriculum resource teacher

WEEKLY READER®
PUBLISHING

Please visit our web site at www.garethstevens.com.
For a free color catalog describing our list of high-quality books,
call 1-800-542-2595 (USA) or 1-800-387-3178 (Canada). Our fax: 1-877-542-2596

Library of Congress Cataloging-in-Publication Data

Benduhn, Tea.
    Oil, gas, and coal / by Tea Benduhn.
       p. cm. — (Energy for today)
    Includes bibliographical references and index.
    ISBN-10: 0-8368-9261-5 — ISBN-13: 978-0-8368-9261-1 (lib. bdg.)
    ISBN-10: 0-8368-9360-3 — ISBN-13: 978-0-8368-9360-1 (softcover)
    1. Fossil fuels—Juvenile literature. I. Title.
TP318.3.B46   2009
665.5—dc22   2008015517

This edition first published in 2009 by
Weekly Reader® Books
An Imprint of Gareth Stevens Publishing
1 Reader's Digest Road
Pleasantville, NY 10570-7000 USA

Senior Managing Editor: Lisa M. Herrington
Senior Editor: Brian Fitzgerald
Creative Director: Lisa Donovan
Designer: Ken Crossland
Photo Researcher: Diane Laska-Swanke
Special thanks to Kirsten Weir

Image credits: Cover and title page: © Stockbyte/Getty Images; p. 5: © Rod Beverley/Shutterstock; p. 6: © Transtock Inc./Alamy; p. 7: © Neil lee Sharp/Alamy; p. 9: © Eray Haciosmanoglu/Shutterstock; p. 10: © AP Images; p. 11: © Frederic J. Brown/AFP/Getty Images; p. 13: © Darla Hallmark/Shutterstock; p. 14: © Paul Glendell/Alamy; p. 15: © Creatas Images/Jupiterimages Unlimited; p. 17: © AbleStock.com/Jupiterimages Unlimited; p. 18: © Mark Schneider/Visuals Unlimited; p. 19: © Visual Mining/Alamy; p. 20: © Jose Gil/Shutterstock; p. 21: © Thinkstock Images/Jupiterimages Unlimited.

Printed in the United States

1 2 3 4 5 6 7 8 9 10 09 08

Table of Contents

Words that appear in the glossary are printed in **boldface** type the first time they occur in the text.

Chapter 1

What Are Fossil Fuels?

Have you ever seen giant dinosaur bones in a museum? Dinosaurs are animals that lived millions of years ago. We know they lived because of **fossils**. Fossils are the remains of ancient animals and plants. Over millions of years, those remains turned into stone. Many types of animals and plants lived long before the time of the dinosaurs. Today, we know about these plants and animals because of fossils.

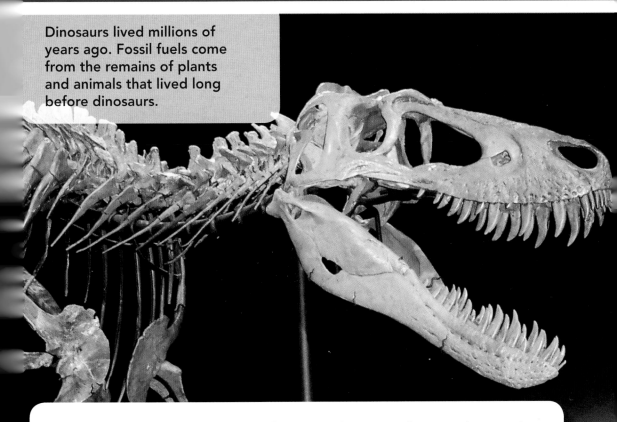

Dinosaurs lived millions of years ago. Fossil fuels come from the remains of plants and animals that lived long before dinosaurs.

Over time, the remains of some plants and animals turn into materials called **fossil fuels**. Coal, oil, and natural gas are fossil fuels. Coal is black and solid, like rock. Oil is a brown liquid. Natural gas is invisible. These fossil fuels provide **energy** that we use to heat our homes, power our lights, and fuel our cars. Most cars run on gasoline, a fuel made from oil—not from natural gas.

Energy is the ability to do work. Everything that can move has energy. Stored energy is called **potential energy**. Moving energy is called **kinetic energy**. Fossil fuels have potential energy. For example, a tank of gasoline in a car has potential energy. When a driver starts a car, the engine burns the gasoline. Burning the gasoline changes its potential energy to kinetic energy. That energy moves the car forward.

A speeding car has a lot of kinetic energy.

Plants get energy from sunlight. Animals get energy from food. When plants and animals die, energy stays stored in them. Millions of years ago, dead plants and animals sank into the ground. As the years passed, they rotted and were buried deeper underground. After millions of years, heat and pressure turned them into fossil fuels. Today, we dig up those fossil fuels to tap into their stored energy.

Fossil fuels are found deep underground. Some oil rigs pump oil from the seafloor.

Chapter 2

Sources of Energy

There are many different sources of energy. Sunlight, wind, and water all contain energy. Sunlight, wind, and water are **renewable resources**. They cannot be used up. The Sun shines every day. The wind is always blowing somewhere on Earth. The amount of water in the world is always the same. We will never use up all the energy in the Sun, water, or wind.

Like cars, airplanes use fuel made from oil.

Today, we get most of our energy from fossil fuels. Power plants burn coal to make electricity that we use to light our homes and schools. Cars and airplanes burn gasoline and other fuels made from oil. Many people burn natural gas to cook or heat their homes. These fossil fuels are **nonrenewable resources**. They cannot be replaced. After fossil fuels burn up, they are gone forever.

The number of cars in the world is going up. As more people use fossil fuels, the price goes up, too.

Have you heard adults talk about the high price of gasoline? The prices of gasoline and other fuels go up over time. The prices go up because fossil fuels are starting to run out. Every day, the world's supply of fossil fuels gets smaller. The world's population grows every year, so more people need energy. Most of that energy comes from fossil fuels.

People in some cities wear special masks to protect them from air pollution.

People need fossil fuels for energy, but using fossil fuels can hurt us. We must burn coal, oil, and natural gas to release their energy. Burning fossil fuels lets off gases that are causing Earth to slowly heat up. This rise in temperature is called **global warming**. The gases from burning fossil fuels also cause **pollution**. Polluted air is dirty and hard to breathe. Polluted air and water can make people sick.

Chapter 3

How Fossil Fuels Work

Fossil fuels form deep underground. Bringing them to the surface is hard work. Coal is found under layers of rock. To mine coal, workers must drill down through the rock. Miners dig a large pit and take out the coal. They also use machines to dig a shaft, or tunnel, deep underground. Machines crush coal into small chunks that are easy to move out of the mine.

Power plants make the electricity we use in our homes and schools. They make electricity from fossil fuels. Power plants burn coal or other fossil fuels to heat water. The heated water turns to steam, like the steam from a teakettle. The whoosh of rising steam turns a **turbine**. The turbine is attached to a machine called a **generator**. The generator turns the turbine's kinetic energy into electricity.

Most power plants in the United States burn coal to make electricity.

13

Oil and natural gas are also found far underground. They are trapped so deep that they are under huge pressure. Workers drill wells to reach oil and gas. The wells release the pressure, and the fuels gush up to the surface. Then they must be sent to factories. Oil is sent through huge pipes or shipped on giant tankers. If oil leaks during the journey, it can harm the environment.

If oil spills into the environment, it can harm birds and other wildlife.

Oil straight from the ground, called **crude oil**, is thick and lumpy. Workers make it pure at an **oil refinery**. Pure oil is made into gasoline. Oil is also used to make many other products, including plastic and crayons! Natural gas is made pure at refineries, too. Then it is turned into liquid. The liquid is piped into homes. People use natural gas for heat and cooking.

Oil is used in many household products, including crayons!

Chapter 4

Energy in the Future

Fossil fuels are not perfect. They make pollution, and they will not last forever. Still, our lives would be very different without fossil fuels. We get 85 percent of our energy from coal, oil, and natural gas. Scientists do not know exactly when fossil fuels will run out. Today, many people are looking for ways to use more renewable energy sources. They are also working to make fossil fuels cleaner.

Today, most of our electricity comes from power plants that burn coal. In the future, our energy may come from renewable sources, such as water, the Sun, and wind. Flowing water can turn turbines to create electricity. Energy from the Sun, called solar energy, can be collected on **solar panels**. Wind farms can gather energy from the blowing wind. More than 30 states make electricity from wind power.

Wind farms collect energy from the blowing wind. In the future, we may get more of our energy from wind.

Scientists are working on ways to make coal a cleaner energy source.

For now, most of our energy comes from fossil fuels. Scientists are working on ways to cut down the pollution that comes from burning fossil fuels. Special filters can block some of the pollution from going into the air. They might also block some of the gases that cause global warming. Scientists are also making cleaner machines that burn fossil fuels without letting off as much pollution.

Cars, trucks, and planes use huge amounts of fossil fuels. Scientists are working on making cars that use cleaner energy sources. Many people are already driving cars that use less gasoline. **Hybrid cars** run on a mix of gasoline and electricity. Other cars use new fuels that are cleaner than gasoline. In the future, more new cars will use cleaner fuels.

Hybrid cars can go farther on one tank of gas than other cars.

Here's a bright idea! Replace older lightbulbs with ones that use much less energy.

Scientists have many other ideas for cutting down on our use of fossil fuels. You don't need to be a scientist to help solve our energy problems, however. The best way to use fewer fossil fuels is to **conserve**, or save, energy. You can help conserve energy at home and in school.

Biking instead of driving is a fun way to save energy. It's also great exercise!

What are some ways you can help save energy? Make sure to turn off lights when you leave a room. Shut off televisions, game systems, and computers when you're done using them. Walk or bike instead of riding in the car. Turn the heat down a bit in the winter. Use a little less air conditioning in the summer. By conserving energy, you can help make our planet a cleaner, greener place.

Glossary

conserve: to save

crude oil: oil that is not pure

energy: the ability to do work

fossils: the remains of plants or animals that lived millions of years ago

fossil fuels: sources of energy, such as oil, gas, and coal, that formed from the remains of plants or animals that lived millions of years ago

generator: a machine that makes electricity or other energy

global warming: the slow rise in Earth's temperature

hybrid cars: cars powered by gasoline and electricity

kinetic energy: energy that is moving

nonrenewable resource: a resource that cannot be used again. Once it is used, it is gone forever. Fossil fuels are nonrenewable resources.

oil refinery: a plant that makes crude oil pure

pollution: harmful materials in the environment

potential energy: energy that is stored

renewable resource: a resource that can be used again. Renewable resources include air, water, sunlight, wind, and plants and animals.

solar panels: devices that collect energy from the Sun

turbine: a machine that turns to create electricity

To Find Out More

Books

Air Pollution. Science Matters (series). Heather C. Hudak (Weigl Publishers, 2006)

Fossil Fuels. Sources of Energy (series). Diane Gibson (Smart Apple Media, 2004)

Web Sites

EIA Energy Kid's Page

www.eia.doe.gov/kids/energyfacts/sources/non-renewable/coal.html

Learn more about how coal forms, how it's mined, and how it's used to make electricity.

Kaboom! Energy

tiki.oneworld.net/energy/energy.html

Find out about many sources of energy, including fossil fuels.

Publisher's note to educators and parents: Our editors have carefully reviewed these web sites to ensure that they are suitable for children. Many web sites change frequently, however, and we cannot guarantee that a site's future contents will continue to meet our high standards of quality and educational value. Be advised that children should be closely supervised whenever they access the Internet.

Index

About the Author

Tea Benduhn writes books and edits a magazine. She lives in the beautiful state of Wisconsin with her husband and two cats. The walls of their home are lined with bookshelves filled with books. Tea says, "I read every day. It is more fun than watching television!"